Snapshots
of Seward

A HISTORY IN PHOTOS

This book is dedicated to
the memory of Sylvia Sexton,
intrepid chronicler of Seward's early years.

Snapshots of Seward – A History in Photos

Published by the Seward Community Library Association, Seward, Alaska

ISBN 978-0-615-33309-0

Library of Congress Control Number: 2009944163

Printed in 2010 in the United States of America

Cover photo: "Young Ladies – Early Days of Seward"
Photo by Sylvia Sexton, courtesy of Seward Community Library.
Back cover photo of Dodie Fillingim as Lady Liberty, courtesy of Seward Community Library
Cover elements: © iStockphoto

Introduction

William Faulkner wrote: "The past is never dead. It's not even past."

If you look carefully at these photos, beyond the surface, beneath the landscape and into the eyes and souls of those who walked our streets, enjoyed our mountain-encircled bay, and lived in our houses before we were born, you'll see yourself.

If you doubt that, turn to page 27 and look at the little girl on the far left in the front row — and convince me children have changed in 100 years. Or, if you question whether the past is dead, take this book with you to the corner of Third and Jefferson, turn to page 39, and look at Millionaire's Row. On a clear day, stand at the August 28, 1903, landing party spot (page 8) and line up the mountains and Fourth of July Creek in the background.

Our past is all around us.

Consider what life was like for soldiers stationed at Fort Raymond, Caines Head, Rugged and Barwell Islands during World War II as you look into the eyes of three of them (page 84). One of them, local resident Jack Turnbull, died as this book was being completed. For many years he represented a local reminder of the sacrifices these soldiers made.

The more I study history, the more I'm convinced that, despite our many human differences, despite our great technological progress, the foundation of our humanity, the great human universals, have not changed. The contexts have changed dramatically, but beneath them you'll find people much like us. We're all born, and we all die. And in between we're all connected with families in some way; some of us marry and have children. We all strive to earn a living, put a roof over our heads, and food on our tables. We all want acceptance and love, and to feel valued. And we want connection — not only to people but to places like Seward and Resurrection Bay.

Look carefully at these photographs. You'll see human universals embedded there. You'll see yourself, and discover that Seward's history isn't dead. It's not even past.

Doug Capra
Seward historian, author and playwright

ACKNOWLEDGMENTS

In 2003 the town of Seward prepared to celebrate its 100 year anniversary. In anticipation of the event, the board members of the Seward Community Library Association, led by Margaret Branson, resolved to gather pictures and stories of the town, and publish them in a book to commemorate the occasion. They began the lengthy process of gathering photos and information, assisted by library staff and others.

For various reasons, the project was not finished in time for the Centennial celebration. It then languished for a while, moving forward in fits and starts, according to the availability of volunteers who had the time to see it through. In 2005 I became the next and final shaper of "The Book." Working from the groundwork already laid, I was able to complete the project in 2010. I would like to thank those who laid that groundwork: the staff at the Seward Community Library (especially Patty Linville, Pam Hermann, Doris Welch and Ryan Reynolds), Lee Poleske of the Resurrection Bay Historical Society, Tim Sczawinski, Kerri Martin and Stan McKnight. Dawn Ernst of Information Design, Inc. was a dream to work with, and her technical expertise and support were invaluable. And of course, thanks go out to the residents of Seward, both past and present, who've lent their memories, stories and photos to this endeavor. Though we were not able to include all the material that was submitted, we applaud the sincere interest of everyone who responded to the call.

Amy Mow
Editor

1902-1915

The Pioneer Years

Eva Lowell *(standing, behind child)*, daughter of Mary Lowell, at one of the family cabins in 1903. Separated from her husband, Frank Lowell, Mary and her children were residing in their cabins on Resurrection Bay when John Ballaine and his party came to establish the town of Seward. She was reportedly paid $4,000 and title to thirty-seven town lots from the sale of her homestead. Recent research has indicated the Lowell's may have settled near the place inhabited by the Russians in 1794, when they built their ship, the *Phoenix*. Prior to that, the area was used by Alutiiq-speaking Alaska Natives for subsistence.

Photo by William A. McPherson, Resurrection Bay Historical Society

HOMESTEAD AT SEWARD IN OCT. 1903.

Herrman William Scheffler, first husband of Alice Lowell (Mary's daughter). The couple had five children, all born in or near Seward, from 1898 to 1904. Alice, who died in a car crash in Tacoma, Washington, in 1965, outlived them all.
Courtesy of Doug Capra

A portion of Alice Lowell's family Bible, recording the births of three of her children. The handwriting is that of her husband, Herrman Scheffler.
Courtesy of Doug Capra

Alice Lowell and Herman Weise, her second husband, in Tacoma, Washington.
Courtesy of Doug Capra

The Ballaine Brothers:
(left to right) Frank, William, and John.

John E. Ballaine, first officer and driving force behind the privately held Alaska Central Railway, was intent on bringing railroad service to the interior of Alaska via Resurrection Bay. The dream began to take shape on August 28, 1903, when Ballaine, his brother Frank and 56 other passengers disembarked on the quiet shores of the future townsite of Seward.

After quickly obtaining land rights, they set about building the wharf and sawmill, key elements in creating the town. Buildings rose, streets were laid out in an orderly fashion, and railroad tracks began their stretch from the shores of Resurrection Bay northward towards Nenana, on the Tanana River hundreds of miles away. Unfortunately, the company could not remain solvent, and in November, 1909, with only 71-1/2 miles of rail laid out, the Alaska Central Railway was forced to sell out. Reincarnated as the Alaska Northern Railway, the railway limped along, suffering a series of setbacks caused by changing governmental policies in development and land rights. Finally, in 1913, the U.S. government took over to complete the line. Now called the Alaska Railroad, it is run by the State of Alaska and continues to provide both passenger and freight service.

Photo by Lillian Gordon,
Resurrection Bay Historical Society

The *Santa Ana* was chartered to bring the first boatload of settlers to the future townsite of Seward in 1903, and returned to Seward many times under the ownership of the Alaska Steamship Company. She was eventually sold, and ended up burning on the Mobile River in Alabama in the 1930's.

Resurrection Bay Historical Society

Part of the original landing party, August 28, 1903.
Photo by Lillian N. Gordon, Resurrection Bay Historical Society

The only means for passengers and goods to arrive in Seward was by boat, so "Steamer Day" was an eagerly anticipated event. Mail, fresh groceries, building materials and passengers all were unloaded at the main dock. While some goods stayed in Seward, most were destined for the gold fields and other communities further north. *Seward Community Library*

A view from the dock towards the fledgling town, circa 1903-1904. The dock was one of the first structures built. Many residents are living in wall tents, as the dense forest on the townsite is cleared and streets begin to take shape. *Seward Community Library*

TAKEN BY MARVEL WILKS PART OF SEWARD ALASKA IN 1905

Seward in 1905. The distinctive two-story log structure on the right was owned by Dr. David H. Sleem. Born in Jerusalem, Dr. Sleem came to the United States and practiced medicine in New York City for ten years before moving north, finally landing in Seward in 1904. An accomplished musician, mapmaker and businessman, Sleem worked both in private practice and as physician for the Alaska Central Railway. In 1908 a fire broke out in "Sleem's Hall," but quick action by the community saved most of the building and his possessions. After the failure of the Alaska Northern Railway, Sleem left Seward for Valdez. He died there in 1913 (Barry 1986; p. 83). *Photo by Marvel Wilks, courtesy of Christina Pichotta*

This photo was taken by William A. McPherson, a photographer employed by the Alaska Central Railway, two months after the city of Seward was founded. The large building on the right, originally the railroad commissary building, was later moved and became part of the Coleman Hotel, run by George Sexton. It sat on the site of the present day Ranting Raven Bakery and Gift Shop. *Photo by William A. McPherson, Resurrection Bay Historical Society*

Surveyors working along the path of the Alaska Central Railway. *Seward Community Library*

Alaska Central Railway train. *Seward Community Library*

Good on Motor Car   No. 955

Alaska Central Railway

Pass *Geo. Sexton*
Subject to conditions printed on back hereof

From *Seward* to *M. 24*

Account *Complimentary*

Expires *when used*

Treasurer.
RECEIVED

Not good unless
Countersigned by

COUNTERSIGNED

Alaska Central Railway
ticket issued to Seward
resident George Sexton.
Seward Community Library

The passenger depot of
the Alaska Northern
Railway (formerly
the Alaska Central
Railway), located at
the foot of Adams
Street, on the bay.
Seward Community Library

Brosius and Noon, one of the first businesses in Seward, around 1910. Cal Brosius and
John Noon provided milling and woodworking services to the fast-growing town.
Seward Community Library

In this early view of Seward (sometime between 1910 and 1916) a portion of Mary Lowell's cabin remains in the center, backed by a large white building. The row of small buildings to the left of center may represent the beginnings of the "Line." This section of town, comprised of the alleyway ("Alley B") between Second and Third Avenues and between Railroad Street on the south and Washington Street on the north, was a sanctioned red-light district. Here, prostitutes catered to the migrant population of seamen, railroad workers, miners, and later, military personnel stationed in Seward.

The women were a vital part of the economy of Seward (as they were in many other Alaskan towns), and the existence of the Line was supported by the townspeople, who were only too happy to confine vice to a single part of town. The prostitutes and madams did not socialize with the regular townswomen, or even appear in town to do their shopping and other errands when the respectable women were likely to be there. In the true Alaskan spirit of being able to reinvent oneself in the Last Frontier, some of the women who came to Seward as prostitutes, or former prostitutes, were able to become proper members of society by marrying local men, or becoming owners of legitimate businesses. Real estate was a popular venture for many. The Line was eventually shut down in 1954, at a time when other such districts around Alaska were shut down, perhaps as a precursor to statehood (Mason 2003). *Seward Community Library*

Early view of Seward from Bear Mountain. *Courtesy of Christina Pichotta*

An early view of Fourth Avenue looking south, circa 1904-1905. *Seward Community Library*

Fourth Avenue looking north from the dock, circa 1915. *Seward Community Library*

The discovery of gold at Nome, Fairbanks, Kantishna, the Klondike and, closer to home, at Hope and Sunrise on the Kenai Peninsula brought thousands of new settlers to Alaska. Many Sewardites also invested in or prospected their own mining claims. Here, Sylvia Sexton and her father, George (*top*), and two unidentified men, pose above a hardrock mine at Mile 44.

Seward Community Library

The Seward Dairy, established in 1915 by F.S. Adelman and Mr. Quilty, was later sold to Henry Leirer. Fresh milk was a highly-valued commodity in Seward before refrigeration and speedy transportation made dairy products more commonplace.
Seward Community Library

Several homesteaders, including William McPherson, Otto Bergstrom and Ole Martin provided much needed fresh produce for the town. Hardy crops of vegetables included potatoes, turnips, carrots, rutabagas, peas, beans, cauliflower, cabbage and lettuce (Barry 1986; 171).
Seward Community Library

Left to right: Hank Lucas, Walter Lodge, and Andy Simons. Simons was a well-known hunting guide on the Kenai Peninsula, and has a mountain named after him there. He was also the second husband of Eva Lowell, daughter of Mary Lowell. Eva's first husband, Harry Revell, was also a well-known hunting guide.
Seward Community Library

Fishing has always been an important part of Seward life, for both sport and subsistence. Here, Sewardite George Sexton displays a large catch of fish.
Seward Community Library

William "Wild Bill" DeWitt was one of Seward's most rugged individuals. Preferring the wilderness to town, he made his living as a provider of meat to local butcher shops and as a hunting guide. He hunted and explored the far reaches of the Kenai Peninsula well into old age. Bill wore his long hair in a single ponytail down his back, and ended his days doing odd jobs around town. He was also a talented photographer.
Seward Community Library

Railroad handcars provided one means of transportation through otherwise roadless terrain. On a fishing trip are pictured, from left to right: George Sexton, Neil Sexton, Claudia Sexton, Mary McNeiley, Mrs. Cappell, Sylvia Sexton, Mr. Cappell, William McNeiley (man in front right unidentified). *Seward Community Library*

Sleds from Brosius and Noon for the
burgeoning sled dog traffic.
Seward Community Library

Dog teams on Fourth Avenue.
Seward Community Library

For years, sled dogs provided the most reliable form of winter transportation throughout Alaska. The U.S. Government employed mushers and their teams to deliver mail throughout the territory after its arrival at the dock in Seward. Unlike today's sled dogs bred for speed, early mushers looked for large, strong dogs with great endurance and the ability to haul heavy loads in poor conditions. Breaking trail was a difficult and tiring job.

Seward Community Library

Rosness, Seward-Kenai Mail Team.
Alaska Shop photo,
courtesy of Christina Pichotta

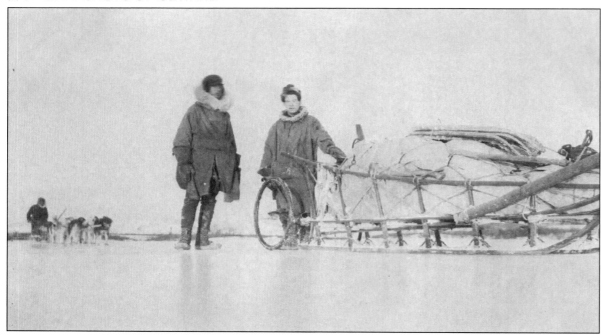

The cyclometer attached to this sled measured the entire distance from Seward to Nome. Long before the famous Iditarod Sled Dog Race came into being, dogs freighted north following several different routes, bringing mail and supplies to the mining communities in the Interior. Once the Alaska Railroad was completed all the way to Nenana, the dog teams were no longer needed out of Seward.
Seward Community Library

Howard Romig, son of Dr. Joseph Romig, and his dog sled.
Courtesy of Kerry Romig

Harry Holben's cutter on Dairy Hill Road. Traveling in the winter in town was sometimes easier than in the spring or summer, when dirt roads became bogged down in mud.
Seward Community Library

A winter excursion.
Seward Community Library

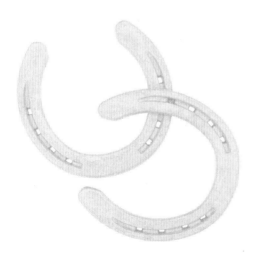

Ladies enjoying a pleasant day fishing. *Seward Community Library*

This photo was captioned: "The children on our block." From left to right are John Van Cleve, Charlotte Van Cleve, Sonny Quinn, Edith Wilson Winter, Margaret Van Cleve and Francis Ballaine. Mr. J.R. Van Cleve (the children's father) was a master mechanic for the Alaska Central Railway in 1905. Francis Ballaine was the son of Frank and Genevieve Ballaine. *Seward Community Library*

An early boom year for babies in Seward. Genevieve Ballaine is second from left. The dress she is wearing was recently "rediscovered" while renovating the Ballaine House on Third Avenue, and is now part of the collection at the Resurrection Bay Historical Society. Mrs. Pedersen, wife of the Methodist minister, is fourth from the left. *Seward Community Library*

Members of the Methodist Church Sunday School on a picnic outing.

Seward Community Library

This postcard photo was donated by Karol Gleason, whose grandfather was in Alaska on a tour of duty with the U.S. Navy in 1913. The view of the main dock shows the naval cruiser *Maryland* in the background. The ship came to Alaska in July 1913 to investigate Alaskan coal deposits as a potential fuel supply for the Pacific fleet, in case of war (Barry 1986; 137). *Seward Community Library*

Baseball game between Seward and the naval crew of the *Maryland*. *Seward Community Library*

1915-1923

Settling In...

ALLOW US TO MINE OUR OWN COAL.

Members of the Seward Commercial Club meet to protest the federal government's move to remove all coal bearing lands in Alaska from staking by private citizens. They lost the battle, and today there are only two private coal claims in Alaska. *Seward Community Library*

The coal-burning torpedo destroyers *John Paul Jones, Perry, Stewart* and *Preble* at the Seward dock in August, 1915. Coal was considered a strategic resource, since most naval vessels, railroads and heavy industries depended on it.

Seward Community Library

Another postcard view from Karol Gleason's grandfather. On the back is written, "Now what do you think of this. We can see just places [sic] like this every day in Alaska. 1913." Note both the long, winding railroad trestle and the short, straight docking pier at the foot of Fourth Avenue. Engines backed onto the trestle which ended parallel to the ship dock, making the off-loading of freight much more convenient. For many years, longshoremen held some of the highest-paying and most stable jobs in Seward.
Seward Community Library

The Alaska Steamship Company freighter *S.S. Seward* at the dock in Seward. *Seward Community Library*

The Alaska Transfer Company (owned by Hoben and Davis) provided local and long distance freight hauling services. Merchandise, both large and small, was offloaded at the docks and brought to local businesses as well as up to Hope and Sunrise on Cook Inlet. Long-time Seward resident Pat Williams identified the horses here as "Mutt and Jeff," named after the popular cartoon characters. Horses were a vital part of the development of Seward for many years.
Seward Community Library

Seward Community Library

The Alaska Transfer Company provided wood delivery service in Seward. Wood was used for heating and cooking in homes and also to power the Alaska Central Railway steam engines.

Seward Community Library

Though mainly thought of as wintertime muscle, dogs were capable of "pulling their weight" in the summer as well.
Seward Community Library

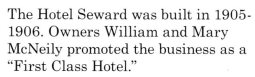

The Hotel Seward was built in 1905-1906. Owners William and Mary McNeily promoted the business as a "First Class Hotel."
Seward Community Library

Interior of the Coleman House, with George Sexton behind the counter. Sexton managed and later purchased the hotel.
Seward Community Library

Interior of the Coleman House, featuring a variety of Native crafts and other Alaskan items. Sylvia Sexton began her Alaska souvenir business here, before moving to a separate building.
Seward Community Library

Group of prominent Seward citizens, taken in the Methodist parsonage (*left to right, top to bottom*): 1. George Sexton (hotel proprietor), 2. William McNeily (hotel proprietor and U.S. Marshal), 3. Dr. Charles T. Dagget (dentist), 4. William P. Henry (proprietor of the Palace Saloon/ Café), 5. Seymour L. Colwell (storekeeper, men's clothing), 6. Christopher C. Shea (game warden), 7. Judge John J. Finnegan (president of Seward Commercial Company), 8. John Noon (pioneer, originator of Seward Commercial Company, businessman). *Seward Community Library*

George Sexton
Seward Community Library

Mrs. Sexton (Claudia Farran Sexton), wife of George, mother of Neil and Sylvia. *Seward Community Library*

Mrs. Louis H. Pederson (wife of the Methodist minister) and children. *Seward Community Library*

Miriam Culbertson Painter (*left*) and Sylvia Sexton (*right*). Miriam came to Seward via Skagway, married Harold Painter, and raised four children in Seward. Her fifth generation descendants are still living here, including granddaughter Dodie who donated this photo.
Seward Community Library, courtesy Doris P. "Dodie" Fillingim

Sylvia Sexton and her father George with a young bear. Sylvia was an avid outdoorswoman and photographer, chronicling many facets of life on the Kenai Peninsula and beyond.
Seward Community Library

Sylvia Sexton in later years in her store. Sylvia began her business selling Alaska souvenirs in the lobby of the Coleman House. Her first store, built in 1907, burned down, but the successor, called "Sylvia's," on Fourth Avenue, continued until the 1940's, serving as a souvenir shop and popular soda fountain (Barry 1986; 81). *Seward Community Library*

Millionaire's Row (north Third Avenue) being built in 1905. These grand homes were built by some of Seward's most prominent families, who believed that some day "one million people would populate the corridor along the railway." The original owners were: (*left to right*) (1) F. H. Stewart, treasurer of Alaska Central Railway, (2) George Winter, ACR official, (3) Murray Burton Holland, ACR General Storekeeper, (4) J.B. Cameron, ACR Chief Construction Engineer (later owned by Dr. Joseph Romig, and eventually, Swan and Wilma Lind), (5) Eugene Hale, Bank of Seward employee (son of F.G. Hale, founder of the Bank of Seward), (6) Frank L. Ballaine, V.P. of Ballaine Brothers Co.

Photo by Evans and Anderson,
Seward Community Library

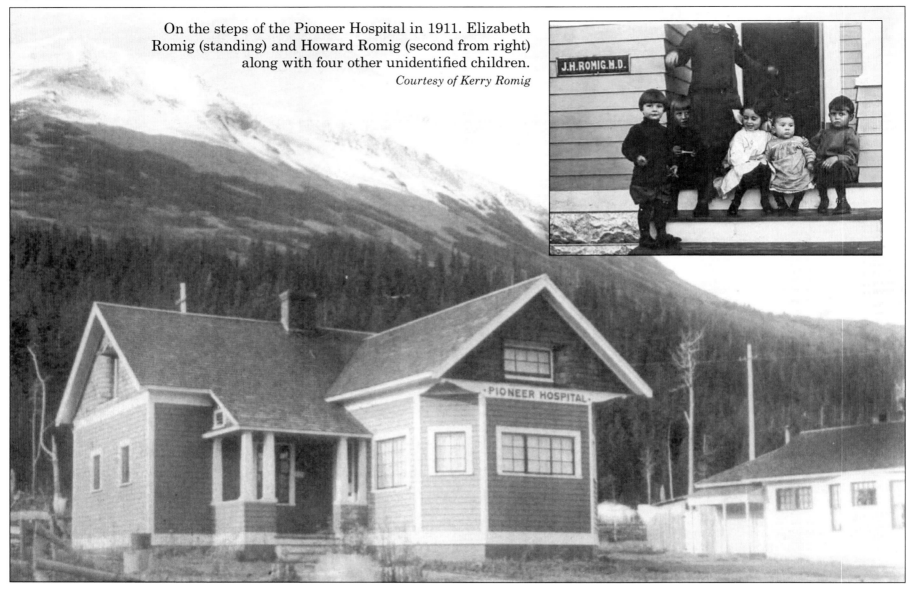

On the steps of the Pioneer Hospital in 1911. Elizabeth Romig (standing) and Howard Romig (second from right) along with four other unidentified children.

Courtesy of Kerry Romig

Dr. Joseph H. Romig opened the Pioneer Hospital on October 13, 1911. The *Seward Gateway* described the hospital's operating room as: "… a model of neatness and cleanliness, equipped with all the instruments and adjuncts necessary. An electric heater affords the desired temperature and a 100-watt electric light makes the room as light as day" (*Seward Gateway*, October 14, 1911). Reportedly, Dr. Romig promised the bachelors he would hire a beautiful, young, trained nurse from the States.

Seward Community Library, courtesy of Wilma Lind

The Frank Ballaine House on Millionaire's Row. The home is currently run as a B & B.
Seward Community Library

Frank Ballaine with wife Genevieve and son Francis. Ballaine played an active role in Seward's development for nearly two decades. He helped his brother John acquire the land on which Seward was built. He was also President of the Seward Water Company and was co-owner of the *Seward Gateway* newspaper.
Seward Community Library

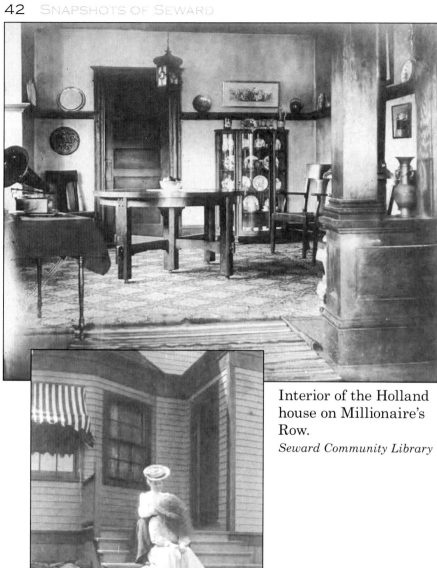

Interior of the Holland house on Millionaire's Row.
Seward Community Library

Florence Burton Holland having her hair dried by Mrs. Burns on the steps of the Holland House.
Seward Community Library

Walking through downtown Seward.
Seward Community Library

Of course, not all dwellings in Seward were as grand as those on Millionaire's Row. However, the owners of these beachfront houses certainly enjoyed a million-dollar view.

Seward Community Library

The Brown and Hawkins Store on Fourth Avenue is the oldest continually operated business in Seward. It has been run by the same family since its inception in 1904. B & H housed a general store, clothing store and the Seward Club Gambling Hall. Today it also houses the Sweet Darlings Candy Shop.

Seward Community Library

The Seward Drug Company was incorporated in 1908 from the former Owl Drug Store. It was eventually bought out by pharmacist Elwyn Swetmann, who also operated Seward Undertaking Parlor with partner Paul C. McMullen. Swetmann, active in many civic organizations, later went on to gain controlling interest in the Bank of Seward. His wife, Viola, a schoolteacher, was also active in the community, and suceeded him as president after his death in 1951. The bank became a branch of the First National Bank of Anchorage in 1952 (Barry 1995: p. 233).
Seward Community Library

Interior of the Seward Drug Company in the mid 1920's. Many of the old bottles lining the upper shelves were still in evidence when the last owner, Jim Woern, sold out in 2006. The entire building was then remodeled by Mark and Yolanda Ifflander as Yoly's Bistro.
Seward Community Library

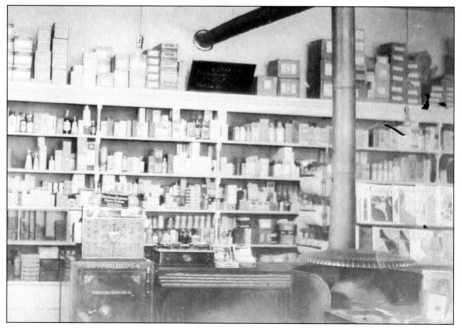

Viola Swetmann.
Seward Community Library

The distinctive Swetmann home was built in 1916 by Gerhard "Stucco" Johnson, a popular local craftsman who specialized in stucco and plasterwork. Johnson built the Spanish Mission-style house for himself and his family, and its original location was up against the bluffs in the part of Seward that is now part of Two Lakes Park. After Johnson sold the house to the Swetmanns it was skidded down the street to its current location at 327 Fifth Avenue. Mrs. Swetmann eventually deeded the house to the Seward Community Library, of which she was a great supporter. *Seward Community Library*

Left to right: Librarian Jackie Deck, Viola Swetmann and Seward Mayor Richard Kirkpatrick at the dedication of Swetmann Hall in the Seward Community Library, 1968.
Seward Community Library

Only a few pilings are left of the once prominent San Juan Fishing and Packing Company. It was located on the shoreline across from the site of a small children's playground today. Work began on the plant in 1917 on land leased from the Alaska Railroad. Initially Chinese laborers were hired to man the plant.

Seward Community Library

A snowy winter on Fourth Avenue.
Seward Community Library

Leon Urbach, his wife Dorothy and sons Kenneth and Larry in front of their store, Urbach's Clothing, which opened in 1915. Larry inherited the store from his father, and today his wife (also named Dorothy) continues to run the family business.
Courtesy of Dorothy Urbach

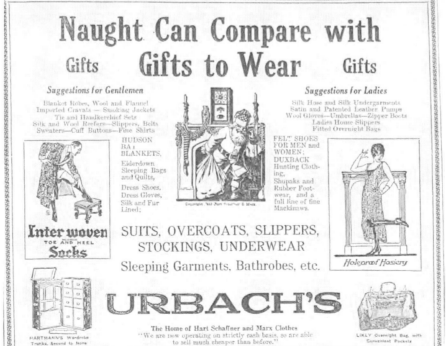

Larry, Dorothy and Kenneth Urbach. Unfortunately, Dorothy died young, of pneumonia. According to the *Gateway* newspaper account: "The funeral cortege was one of the largest ever to have been formed in the city; this, in the face of a blasting-cold north wind. Automobiles lined both sides of Fourth Avenue. Local firms suspended business for the day, and public schools closed, in respect to the memory of Mrs. Leon Urbach" (*Seward Gateway*, December 7, 1933).
Seward Community Library

Urbach's ad from the *Seward Gateway*, 1925.
Courtesy of Dorothy Urbach

"Motoring" was a popular pastime among Seward residents who enjoyed exploring the surrounding areas for fishing, berrypicking, hiking and other excursions. *Seward Community Library*

Will Rogers (*left*) and Leon Urbach (*right*) on a road tour north of Seward, 1935. An amiable and enthusiastic man, Urbach could always be found doing something interesting. *Courtesy of Dorothy Urbach*

New Year's Eve party 1924-1925. *Courtesy of Dorothy Urbach*

Travelers came by steamship to explore Alaska in style.
A picture of Seward graced the front of this menu from
the *S.S. Yukon*, July 29, 1933.
Courtesy of Dorothy Urbach

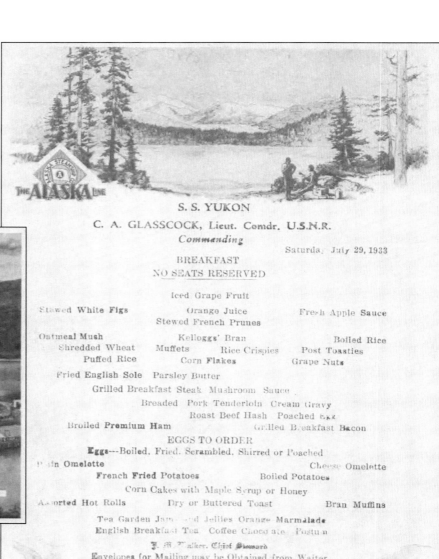

THE ALASKA LINE

S. S. YUKON

C. A. GLASSCOCK, Lieut. Comdr. U.S.N.R.
Commanding

Saturday, July 29, 1933

BREAKFAST
NO SEATS RESERVED

Iced Grape Fruit

Stewed White Figs   Orange Juice   Fresh Apple Sauce
Stewed French Prunes

Oatmeal Mush   Kelloggs' Bran   Boiled Rice
Shredded Wheat   Muffets   Rice Crispies   Post Toasties
Puffed Rice   Corn Flakes   Grape Nuts

Fried English Sole   Parsley Butter

Grilled Breakfast Steak Mushroom Sauce

Breaded Pork Tenderloin Cream Gravy
Roast Beef Hash   Poached Egg
Broiled **Premium** Ham   Grilled Breakfast Bacon

EGGS TO ORDER
Eggs---Boiled, Fried, Scrambled, Shirred or Poached
Plain Omelette   Cheese Omelette
French **Fried** Potatoes   Boiled Potatoes
Corn Cakes with Maple Syrup or Honey
Assorted Hot Rolls   Dry or Buttered Toast   Bran Muffins

Tea Garden Jams and Jellies Orange Marmalade
English Breakfast Tea   Coffee Chocolate Postum

F. M. Walker, Chief Steward

Envelopes for Mailing may be Obtained from Waiter
Please Refrain from Smoking in the Dining Room

Hoben Park, next to the train station, was a beautiful and welcoming sight for incoming passengers off the steamships. Originally called Nile Park, it was built largely by contributions made by local businessman Harry Hoben, who owned the Arcade Building across the street. *Seward Community Library*

President Harding in front of St. Peter's Episcopal Church.
Seward Community Library

As part of his ambitious "Voyage of Understanding" tour across the United States (promoting his policies and idea of a World Court to provide international justice), President Warren G. Harding came to Seward on July 13, 1923. He and his party spent several enjoyable days visiting the local sights and meeting the residents of Seward. Sadly, Harding died shortly after completing the Alaskan leg of his tour, and while the end of his administration was marked by allegations of graft and corruption, the people of Seward remembered him fondly (Barry 1993; 31-32).

Harding's motorcade. The recently completed Arcade building can be seen in the background. Owners of the three-story building, Harry Hoben and Al Davis, provided every modern convenience for the six 4- and 5-room upper floor apartments, including a central vacuum system. Early tenants included Leon Urbach and his sister and brother-in-law, Hugh and Esther Dougherty. The lower floors were occupied by offices of the Alaska Steamship Company and the Resurrection Bay Lumber Company. The Gateway Publishing Company occupied a large part of the basement floor. The building was described as an "all-Seward product," as everything from the planning to construction to building materials were of local origin (Barry 1993; 97-98). The original Arcade burned down in the fire of November 23, 1941, which claimed almost half of the business district in Seward. It was rebuilt shortly after, and survived for many years, but was eventually torn down in 2006. *Seward Community Library*

The Bank of Seward building, built in 1906, and the Van Guilder Hotel at the corner of Fourth and Adams Streets. The concrete block bank has been stuccoed in Art Deco style in this 1920's photo. The two-story log home of Dr. David H. Sleem can be seen to the right of the bank. *Seward Community Library*

Leroy Vincent "L.V." Ray, a highly respected attorney, arrived in Seward in 1906 at the invitation of F.G. Hale, president of the Bank of Seward. He was quickly appointed Assistant District Attorney, and traveled frequently to Valdez, where he met and married a local belle, Hazel Sheldon. The Rays had two children, Hazel Patricia Ray and Lee Vincent Ray. While in Seward, Ray served as City Attorney for Seward, was elected mayor six times, was elected Senator of the Third District and became president of the first Territorial Senate from 1913 through 1915. His office, located in the rear of the Harriman Bank Building (at the corner of Fifth and Adams), is now called the L.V. Ray Building.
Courtesy of Pat Williams

Hazel (Sheldon) Ray, 1965. *Courtesy of Pat Williams*

St. Peter's Episcopal Church, built in 1906, was the first church building in Seward. It still stands today in excellent condition on its original site at the corner of Second and Adams.

Seward Community Library

The original Sacred Heart Catholic Church was built in 1909-1910 on a lot donated by John E. Ballaine.

Seward Community Library

Originally built as the Seward Methodist Church in 1916, this building was sold in 1949 and became Resurrection Lutheran Church. The Lutherans owned the building until 1993, when it went into private ownership, and it now houses a popular coffee house and gallery called Resurrect Art.

Seward Community Library

The Methodists received this church building from the U.S. Army base at Fort Raymond. It was moved to the corner of Fourth Avenue and Church Street in 1946. Sadly, the building was destroyed by fire on December 26, 1994.

Seward Community Library

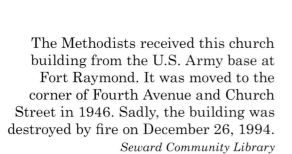

Sacred Heart Catholic Church and rectory as they appeared in the 1930's. A new church, parish hall and rectory was built in 1965. The old building burned down in 1989.

Seward Community Library

The interior of Sacred Heart Catholic Church decorated for Easter.

Seward Community Library

The Laughlin family: (*left to right*) Geraldine, Wilbur, Genevieve, Laura, Wilma and, in front, Alberta (who married Barton Stanton and continued to live in Seward until her death). *Courtesy of Wilma Lind*

Wilbur and Laura Laughlin at their home in Seward. The old Federal Building is in the background. *Courtesy of Wilma Lind*

Wilma Lind

(Excerpted from Sharon Bushell's "Alaskana" column, *Anchorage Daily News*, Sunday, April 21, 2002.)

"I was born in 1909 and raised on a farm in eastern Kansas. As there were no brothers, my older sister and I became Dad's [Wilbur Laughlin] farmhands, milking cows and working in the fields.

We lost our farm in '25 and came to Alaska in '26. We settled seven miles outside of Seward in a house that my uncle (George Laughlin) had built. He lived right next to us, but other than that we were pretty isolated. Our other neighbors were two to three miles away. To make sure we didn't starve that first winter, Mom [Laura Laughlin] picked gallons of blueberries and canned lots of salmon.

Dad went to work cutting ties, then he was hired to work on the section for the Alaska Railroad. My oldest sister taught at the Woodrow School at Mile 7, where I did part-time janitor work. I would then walk over the hill to Bear Lake, where I ran the cutoff saw in the mill. Later I worked at Sylvia's, the soda fountain and candy store in town.

There was a crew of men working on a bridge at Bear Creek. They would occasionally come over to our house, and we'd all play cards. That's how I met my husband, Swan Lind (an immigrant from Sweden).

Swan and I married in 1928 and built a house at Mile 7. He and his partner Carl got a job working for the railroad, cutting ties at Mile 10, which they then hauled to Mile 12. They built a log cabin, and I became the cook. We did that for three years. Our oldest daughter spent her first Christmas in that cabin.

When that job was done we moved back to our home and started raising and selling chickens. We also sold potatoes and carrots by the burlap bag full and gallons of strawberries. I used to deliver eggs around town in our Ford sedan. Meanwhile, Swan had gotten a road-maintenance job and later worked as a longshoreman.

Our children went to school in town. We always drove them in; we never thought of asking anybody to furnish us a school bus. In winter, if you planned to stay someplace any length of time, you'd have to take something to cover your car or else start it once in a while. And of course we always used chains.

During World War II Swan and the other local men took turns patrolling the waterline at night. In case the Japanese invaded, a committee had worked out a plan that they were going to evacuate us to the section house at Mile 12. It was a pretty frightening thought. I put the battery for our truck on a sled and made sure it was charged; we were all ready to go. Finally, Swan insisted that the girls and I go Outside, so we went back to Kansas. We only stayed one year, and as soon as we were allowed back in, we came back.

Swan passed away in 1953. Our two girls [Joanne and Jeanette] were old enough to be on their own, and our son, Ronald, was 8 years old. I started doing lots of baby-sitting. Then in 1959, I did something very uncharacteristic: I bought a setnet site on Nikiski Beach. How I ever had the nerve to do that I'll never know. I didn't know a thing about fishing. I could get seasick sitting on the porch watching the waves.

Ronald and I built a little punt in our basement from purchased plans, and I bought a jeep and various fishing apparatus, kegs, nets, etc. Our site was about two miles down the beach from Arness Dock.

When I bought the site it had a cabin, which was on the beach. One winter we had a real bad storm, which washed the cabin away. We built a second one on the beach, which also washed

The Laughlins (*left to right*): Geraldine, Laura, Genevieve and Alberta in their picnic togs ready to enjoy Alaska's outdoors, about 1927.
Courtesy of Wilma Lind

Wilma with George Laughlin's automobile, about 1926. The front tires are solid rubber with holes through them.
Courtesy of Wilma Lind

Ronald, the third Lind to enjoy the wicker baby buggy. The buggy is now in the Seward Museum along with the children's wicker doll buggy. *Courtesy of Wilma Lind*

The Lind home today, with an enclosed porch and other remodeling. Swan and Wilma Lind bought the former Cameron house and Pioneer Hospital (*see page 40*) in 1938 for $1,600. In 1946 they sold their original house at Mile 7, along with some outbuildings and 13 acres, for $3,000. *Courtesy of Wilma Lind*

away. Then we decided maybe we should build up on the hill. Ronald fished with me until he needed to earn more money for college, at which time I hired a young boy, Mike Lantz, to help me. I learned to tie all the necessary knots and strap kegs, but I never learned to mend nets. I always said they can't blame me if there's not enough escapement, as I'm sure plenty of fish went through my nets.

We also built a smokehouse from scrap lumber and cool-smoked salmon, which I sold commercially through Seward Trading. I never made much money fishing, but we had a good time and there was always plenty of fish to eat. It was an interesting experience and I'm glad I did it, but by '69 it was just too much hard work, so I sold the site.

When Swan and I were living at Mile 7, there was a house in town that I always admired, the Romig house. It had been a hospital at one time. In 1938 we heard that the owners were going to sell it, so I told Swan to hurry into town and buy it if he could; I really wanted that house. I have lived here now for 64 years and can't imagine living anywhere else.

Over the years, there was a succession of children who passed through my home and became my temporary children, so to speak. They were mostly kids who were about to graduate and wanted to attend their last year of high school in Seward. They came from all over: Cordova, Girdwood, Hope, Homer. It was such a pleasure to share my home with them; I've discovered that young people are good at helping you stay young."

Wilma passed away in 2007.

1924-1940

Seward Grows

These colonists arrived in Seward in early May, 1935, looking to homestead in the Matanuska Valley. They took the train to Palmer, where each family was assigned a tent. On May 23rd a drawing was held to determine which homesite tracts they would receive.

Seward Community Library

Pat Williams and Dennis
(age 2), next to the
wheelhouse of the
S.S. *Starr*, 1938.
Courtesy of Pat Williams

Eva Anderson and daughter
Shirley arriving in Seward by
steamship, August, 1923.
Courtesy of Margaret Anderson

Johanna, John and John Paulsteiner, 1924. John Paulsteiner arrived in Alaska in 1916 and worked for the Alaska Railroad and the railroad sternwheeler *Midnight Sun* on the Yukon River. He met and married his wife, Johanna, while on a trip to Germany in 1922. Settling down in Seward, John worked at the Cal Brosius lumber company, as a longshoreman at the Seward Dock, and then operated a fish and meat market on the Seward dock. In 1941 he bought out the lumber company from Cal Brosius's widow, and later operated a propane supply company. Paulsteiner left Seward, but returned with his second wife in the early 1970's. After suffering a stroke, he ended his days at the Sitka Pioneer Home in 1976. Paulsteiner published a booklet of reminiscences entitled "Seward, Alaska, the Sinful Town on Resurrection Bay" in his eighties, and his daughter, Mary (Barry), went on to become Seward's most respected and prolific historian. *Seward Community Library*

Playing in the backyard between the Shea house (*left*) and Manthey house (*right*) on Second Avenue, 1920's. Note the bear hide drying on the wall of the Shea house. *Courtesy of Seward and Barbara Shea*

Alaska Railway Depot, late 1920's. The Alaska Railway Depot in Seward was built in 1916, after the U.S. government purchased the former Alaska Central/Alaska Northern Railway and its right of ways. Thousands of visitors and new residents to Alaska passed through this building at the start of their Alaskan adventures. Both the original Alaska Central Depot and its successor were located at the end of Adams Street. The new depot was moved to its present location on Railway Avenue in 1928. The fully-restored building is one of the few ARR depots left; the other two are located in Wasilla and Nenana. It is currently being used as office space by the Alaska SeaLife Center. *Seward Community Library*

The Alaska Railway's engine house and machine shop, built in the early 1920's. *Courtesy of Barbara Shea*

Dock workers rest after unloading a Standard Oil tank car from a steamship, around 1925. The coming of tank cars signaled the beginning of Alaska's transition from wood and coal power to an economy and lifestyle largely centered around oil. In the background, an Alaska Railroad steam-operated crane places bundles of railroad ties on a flat car. Much of the heavy equipment used by the railroads came north after being used to build the Panama Canal. *Seward Community Library*

The Jesse Lee Home

The Jesse Lee Home originated in Unalaska as a mission-run home for Native Alaskan children. Under the direction of the Methodist Church, it was moved to Seward in 1924, to take advantage of the better climate and access to year-round transportation for goods and services. One hundred acres of land was donated by the city and by private citizens. The town of Seward came together for the ground-breaking:

"Mayor L.V. Ray proclaimed a general holiday for May 21, 1925 so all of Seward's citizens could be at the Home location and help clear the grounds. A large crowd turned out for the job, carrying grub hoes and saws. Many walked, while those with cars donated transportation. Powdermen prepared charges and blew out the obstructions. Brosius and the Alaska Transfer furnished caterpillar tractors and horse teams to pull stumps. Chef Mel Holben served the workers a lunch of

Children reading at the Jesse Lee Home.
Photo by Carrie Ida Pierce, Seward Community Library

sandwiches, beans and hot dogs. By 5 p.m., the building site was cleared, large piles of stumps and brush were burned, and the crowd went home. Forty men built a road from the main highway to the Home. A large force of men constructed the Home buildings through the summer. In August, Gerhard Johnson and his crew applied the stucco."

Over the years, the Jesse Lee Home served hundreds of children, offering them not just food and shelter, but a place to learn and grow. Aside from their schooling and regular church services, the children participated in all aspects of the daily chores, from laundry, farming, mending and cleaning to tending the furnace and feeding the various food animals such as cattle, rabbits and chickens. The children often ventured into town, and while it may have been difficult for them to establish relationships with the "Town Kids," they enjoyed themselves nonetheless. Benny Benson, a boy from Chignik who later became famous for designing the Alaska Flag, related:

"Life at the mission was not all work. We enjoyed the many recreations to be had at our Seward home. I loved to swim and got to be a good swimmer at the home. We had ball games and as boys, fishing was a great sport. Of course, the annual Mt. Marathon race was a challenge for all of us boys. Usually it was a boy at the home who came in first. I managed to come in second myself one year. It was a grueling climb to the top and a person had to be well conditioned to finish the race. It was great fun just hiking in the woods and enjoying the many other pleasures of outdoor life… The boys at the Jesse Lee Home had a few more liberties than the girls. We could go into the downtown area quite often unchaperoned and it was real fun exploring the docks, the railroad terminal and looking in the store windows" (Barry 1995; 65).

The Jesse Lee Home finally closed its doors in Seward due to extensive damages caused by the Good Friday Earthquake in 1964. It reopened in Anchorage in 1966, and has been operating under the auspices of Alaska Children's Services since 1970.

The Jesse Lee Home was closed during World War II from 1942 to 1945. The buildings, painted with a camouflage pattern to confuse Japanese bombers, were used by the Army's Fort Raymond. *Seward Community Library*

The Jesse Lee Home, about 1940. *Seward Community Library*

Benny Benson's original submission
to the Alaska flag competition.
Courtesy of Alaska State Museum, Juneau

In 1926 the American Legion sponsored a contest to design a flag for the Territory of Alaska. Open to schoolchildren around the state, the winning design was produced by 13-year-old Benny Benson, a resident of the Jesse Lee Home in Seward. Benson was rewarded with a gold watch and a $1000 scholarship, which he later used to complete a diesel engine training course for mechanics, in Seattle. Benson went on to become one of Alaska's most well-known Native sons. Living out his later years in Kodiak, Alaska, he became a regular guest of honor at Anchorage's Fur Rondy, and was honored many times over for his achievement.

Original letter of congratulations
from the American Legion to
Benny Benson.
Seward Community Library

THE AMERICAN LEGION
DEPARTMENT OF ALASKA
JUNEAU, ALASKA

April 26, 1927.

Benny Benson,
Seward Mission School,
Seward, Alaska.

Dear Benny:

This letter is to officially notify you that you have won first place in The American Legion's Alaska Flag Design Contest, sponsored by the posts comprising the Department of Alaska. And we all wish to congratulate you for being so honored.

The watch, which will have your design enameled on the back of it, has been ordered. However, it will take some little time to get the work done on it, so please exercise patience with us. It will be a beautiful present and one worth waiting a little while for.

An appropriation has been made by the lower body of the Legislature for a trip to be made by you to Washington to present our first flag to the President. Also, little flags will be provided for distribution as souvenirs. I am sure both houses of the Legislature will adopt your design for making Alaska's Flag; in fact, the House has already done so.

With best wishes to you, I am,

Yours very truly,

(J. T. PETRICH)
Adjutant.

jtp

The newly completed "Seward School" in 1914. For many years classes were held in a variety of locations all over town. Though enrollment fluctuated according to the fortunes of the times, the school year of 1914-1915 began with an impressive 24 primary students (later increasing to 32) and 24 grammar and high school students (Barry 1993; 139). Used as a school until 1929, the building became home to Seward General Hospital in 1930. A new school, the "William H. Seward" public school, was able to accommodate additional children of high school age from the Jesse Lee Home. There was also a small school at Woodrow (Mile 7) and a Territorial School, "Bayview," that taught up to the eighth grade.
Seward Community Library

The William H. Seward School was completed in 1929. Seward students gathered here to attend first grade through high school. In 1970 the Alaska Vocational Technical School (AVTEC) began using the building.
Seward Community Library

Arlene Rheingans
(née: Lisa Augustine)

"My parents, Joyce and Ervin Rheingans, first glimpsed Seward from the deck of the Alaska steamship *Victoria* in late March, 1937. After weathering much of the Great Depression in Salinas, California, the two former Minnesota farm kids heard there was gold to be found in the streams of Alaska. They joined a syndicate of thirteen men, including some young fellows from Salinas who had mined in Alaska the previous summer. My folks' share of the operation cost $700.

Despite Mom's having chicken pox, the ten fortune hunters traveled first via train to Moose Pass and then by Caterpillar, sled and snowshoes on to Hope. They spent a night at Oscar Dahl's cabin on Summit Lake. Their mine was located some five miles above Hope on Summit Lake. When the previous year's cook failed to show up, Mom was designated culinary duties. After an entire summer of hard work and primitive living, when the final "clean up" arrived, it was disappointing. My folk's portion of the profits wasn't enough to secure their passage back Outside.

That winter Mom and Dad trapped with the Mathison brothers on Chickaloon Flats, and when summer finally arrived they shared the Mathison's cabin in Hope. Dad tried his hand at mining once more, but with a different crew. He was nearly killed that fall while trying to start an old dragline that had been abandoned in Sunrise and which the men had "walked" to their mine. He had apparently set the magneto timing too fast, and when he kicked down on the crank, it kicked back right between his legs and lifted him up to the ceiling of the cab. He was knocked unconscious and fell, straddling a narrow plank before crashing into the pit below. His injuries were too severe to risk the arduous trip to Seward, so Mom and Emma Clark did their best with hot and cold compresses and morphine.

Arlene Rheingans in Hoben Park, mid-1940's.
Courtesy of Lisa Augustine (née: Arlene Rheingans)

My mother conceived as soon as Dad recovered from his injuries. The last week of May Mom rode to Seward with Dennie McCart who ran the Hope Truckline to await the baby's arrival. They were both scared to death the baby would arrive en route, but were spared that trauma. Mom stayed with Mr. and Mrs. Sears who lived near the hospital. After a five day labor, I was finally wrestled into the world on June 5, 1939. Dr. Ray Bannister had an infected finger, so another doctor made the delivery. The miners called me the Dragline Kid, and my father called me that for the rest of his life. I recently published my memoirs of growing up on the Kenai Peninsula titled *The Dragline Kid.*

In 1942 we moved from Hope to Seward. Dad longshored on the docks and Mom managed a rooming house on Fifth Avenue called the Portland Arms. The business was owned by Sam Romack and his half brother, Tony Parish. They had recently converted an old warehouse into the boarding house with ten rooms and an apartment for the manager.

Mom cleaned and rented the rooms and kept the books. When the Army built a base called Ft. Raymond in Seward, several hundred young fellows arrived and Seward began living up to its wild and wooly reputation. Until the base was completed the GIs hung around the streets with nothing constructive to do. According to Mom's memory, many of them simply "drank, fought, picked up girls if they could and made real pests of themselves." Just down the alley from us a six-year-old girl was attacked and the women of Seward became increasingly nervous. Mom's friend always carried an ax when she came to call. [Many residents agreed that the war years saw an increase in crime, and that often people would "just disappear," never to be seen again.]

An older couple we called Mama and Papa McGowan often took me to the little park by the railroad station to play with bunnies that lived there, and our boarders bribed me with candy to stand on the stairs and recite nursery rhymes and "pieces." Eventually the candy consumption got so out of hand that Mom pinned a note to the back of my dress: "Do not feed me or give me candy!"

Mom began frequently seeing men go past her kitchen window and up the stairs to the second floor. She had recently rented a room to a single man from Anchorage, so she went to investigate. Her knock was answered by two young women who turned out to be "ladies of the evening." The police quickly escorted them to the train.

In late fall a fire broke out in some buildings behind the Portland. Mom recalled that three buildings on Fourth Avenue burned, leaving "an awful looking gap" on that block. Our renters were stoking their heaters to the red hot point and Mom was afraid they'd burn the place down. So we left the perils of big, brawling Seward and returned to the relative peace and quiet of Hope.

During our remaining years in Alaska we came to Seward for yearly medical and dental exams. I fondly recall ice cream cones from Sylvia's and the thrill of visiting The Alaska Shop and Brown and Hawkins. I'll admit to an inordinate sense of pride in being a native Alaskan. And I'm delighted to claim Seward, Alaska, as my birthplace."

Lisa Augustine, August, 2002.

Sol Urie

Sol Urie was born in New York City in 1901 and, after a stint in Germany during World War I, came to Alaska with the military in 1918. He specialized in communications, and worked with the Washington Alaska Military Cable and Telegraph Service (WAMCATS). He was first stationed in Fairbanks and along the Richardson Trail, which paralleled the telegraph line. He then transferred to Valdez, where he met and married Hilma Hihnala in 1925. When the WAMCATS headquarters moved to Seward, Sol and his growing family (children Wilna Lee and Martin) came along. Their younger children, Sidney and Sanna, were born in Seward. Sol quickly became involved in many activities around town, from softball to sportfishing, and also played drums and trombone with the military and town bands. Trained in his youth as a baker, Sol went to work at and eventually bought the Seward Bakery (Barry 1995; 134). His daughter Sanna recalls:

"My Dad and Mom bought the Seward Bakery in 1934. This was the beginning of a family business and we all worked at whatever we were capable of doing. As soon as I could get on a step stool, I washed pots and pans, and from there to cleaning, frying donuts, wrapping bread. As I grew older, I waited on customers out front and, of course, that was the best. We sang, composed rhymes, danced and made the hot, hard work fun in the Bake Shop. Mom did the accounting and was the one who was called "The Boss.""

Sol Urie, owner of the Seward Bakery, stands behind the counter displaying an assortment of fresh bread, rolls and pies. *Courtesy of Sanna LeVan*

Dad built a cabin at Snug Harbor, on Kenai Lake, and every chance he could would spend time there. One time he thought my brother Sid and I could set the bread and bake it, so we were left in charge. Well, a disaster occurred – we left out something, and we had lead bread! Mrs. Hagen had lots of food for the ducks and chickens! During the war (World War II) Dad tried to enlist, but was told that he was not healthy enough for service. Turns out, the military wanted him to stay and bake them their bread! We supplied Fort Raymond with 1,000 loaves a day, working round the clock. They sent us some soldiers to help out with the baking."

After World War II, Sol sold the Bakery, moved full-time to the cabin, and worked for Odom Company (a wholesaler of liquor, soft drinks and other goods). He moved back to Seward in 1952 and opened Solly's bar in the old Brosius building. Eventually, Sol and Hilma followed their sons to Kodiak, where Hilma died in 1974. Sol spent a few years in Hawaii, but returned to Kodiak where he passed away in 1982. His daughter Sanna, who married Duane LeVan (soon after meeting him at Sylvia's soda fountain) still resides in Seward today.

Wilna Lee later became very active in Alaska politics. After traveling with her husband, geologist John McAnerney, she returned to her home state, and served as a member of the Seward City Council and as Seward's mayor. She was appointed State Commissioner of Community and Regional Affairs under Governor Jay Hammond. Wilna Lee McAnerny made several "firsts" for women in Alaskan politics and community affairs, including chairing the Alaska Municipal Bond Bank, the State Senate Adhoc Committee on Oil and Gas Municipal Property taxation, and served on many other boards as well (Barry 1995; 231).

"The 3rd Avenue house" with (*left to right*): Martin Urie, Seward Shea, Sidney Urie, Wilna Lee Urie, Sanna G. Urie, Francis Shea.
Courtesy of Sanna LeVan

Like many Alaskan towns, Seward has long had a fondness for (and a great need for) indoor sports such as basketball. In 1925 the Seward Athletic Club rented the Dreamland Hall, and transformed it into an athletic hall with permanent regulation markings for indoor baseball, basketball, volleyball and handball. In 1926 Seward had enough women players to form two teams, the Gateway Girls and the Marathon Maids. In the following years, tournaments became more elaborate, with communities along the railbelt and elsewhere in Alaska participating (Barry 1995; 76-77).

Wilma Shellhorn (top row, far right)) began one of Seward's basketball "dynasties." Wilma (who was born in Seward in 1916) played, as did her grandson Willie Giles, her three granddaughters Vicki Giles (Loomis), Dina Giles and Kathy Condit (Ryan), and grandchildren Warren, Devin and Lara Loomis. Vicki and her also-Seward-born husband Byron Loomis helped organize and coach the first Urbach's youth basketball league in 1995. Byron played men's league basketball for over 20 years. The Urbach league continues today as a popular training ground for young ball players.

Long-time Seward resident Willard Dunham recalled the early days playing basketball in Seward. As part of the "railbelt" communities, Seward

Girls basketball team 1932-1933.
Courtesy of Vicki Loomis

teams would travel by train to play their games. The small gym they used in Seward had a balcony so close to the hoops that oftentimes the spectators couldn't resist "knocking a few players heads" against the backboards when they came up for a shot. When they traveled to Anchorage, they played on a small, narrow "cigar court" built where the Snow Goose restaurant now stands.

Swimmers at First Lake, late 1920's.
Also known as "Harriman Lake," the
popular swimming hole once sported two
spring diving boards and dressing rooms
for women and men (Barry 1995).
Courtesy of Christina Pichotta

Courtesy of Judi Christiansen

Seward baseball team, 1909. *Seward Community Library*

Baseball was enthusiastically played by early Sewardites. The town had many teams, including the Northern Baseball team, the Branch team, the Fat and Lean teams, the Roughnecks and the Regulars. As competition grew, women's and children's teams formed as well.

Games were played at Branch Park, which was set up north of town. It was enlarged to accommodate croquet, tennis and other activities. Grandstands were set up for the spectators. The local teams not only played against each other, but took on teams from visiting ships and from Valdez and Cordova. The excursions between Seward and Valdez developed into great occasions, with a hundred or more people traveling by ship for the games and accompanying festivities (Barry 1986).

Winter equipment piled outside this cabin includes snowshoes, skis and toboggans, which were used for recreation, hunting and general travel. *Seward Community Library*

Ladies playing tennis outside the Methodist parsonage near Third and Adams Streets.
Seward Community Library

Patterson Taxi, owned and operated by Bill Patterson, boasted one of the earliest automobiles in Seward, around 1922. At the time, there were 24 private vehicles and 12 trucks in town. Motoring was then, as now, a source of entertainment as well as business, though the roads were short and in poor condition. The road to Kenai Lake was completed in 1923, greatly expanding opportunities for automobile touring in the spring and summer. Winters were still a problem, as the roads went unplowed. During the winter, transportation north of Seward reverted to dog team (Barry 1993).

Seward Community Library

One of the four Douglas World Cruiser aircraft moored in Resurrection Bay in April of 1924. Three of these U.S. Army aircraft went on to became the first to fly around the earth. (The fourth crashed en route from Chignik to Dutch Harbor, and while the crew were unharmed, the airplane was destroyed. Parts of it were recovered, and eventually taken to the Alaska Historical and Transportation Museum in Palmer, Alaska.) It took them 175 days at an average speed of 75 mph to fly 35,000 miles over 28 countries, operating interchangeably for land or water landings. The flyers rested for the night at the Van Gilder Hotel before continuing on their journey.

Seward Community Library

Boating has always been a popular pastime in the Seward area, for both recreation and fishing.

Courtesy of Judi Christiansen

Seward Community Library

1941-1958

The War Years

With the advent of World War II, many
local men joined the armed services.

Courtesy of Seward and Barbara Shea

An early view of Fort Raymond, looking east, 1941. Before more substantial quarters were built, enlisted men lived in platform tents.

Seward Community Library

In the years 1940-1941 (preceding World War II) increased attention was paid to Alaska as a location of military importance, due to its proximity to Japan and Russia. As Alaska's farthest north, year-round ice-free port with railroad service to the interior of Alaska, Seward played a vital role. Shipments of materials and military personnel arrived by boat from the Lower 48 on their way inland to military installations in Anchorage and Fairbanks. During the war years seven docks were in use on the waterfront.

The military had a huge presence, and contributed greatly to the town's infrastructure by building roads, airfields, docks and other vital improvements. As a result of this increased activity, Seward's population swelled from about 700-800 to over 3500 (mostly due to military units stationed there) during the war years, and the once sleepy town became invigorated. During the summer of 1941 work began on Fort Raymond, Seward's own military installation. Located 1-1/2 miles north of town on land near the Jesse Lee Home (which had been evacuated for the war), Fort Raymond began with tents erected on wooden platforms, which were soon followed by barracks of a more semi-permanent nature. The white stucco buildings vacated by the Jesse Lee staff and students were painted with trees for camouflage, and put to use by the Army. The Fort became home for the various units whose task it was to safeguard the harbor and Resurrection Bay from enemy infiltration. Gun emplacements and searchlight positions were built all along the bay, from Seward south to Fort McGilvray (Caines Head North and South Beaches), Rocky Point, Rugged Island, Patsy Point, Lowell Point and other locations. The remains of these installations can still be seen today, particularly at Caines Head State Recreation Area.

With the war winding down, Fort Raymond was gradually phased out, and was put into caretaker status in December 1944. Some of the buildings were converted to a sanitorium for tuberculosis, while another portion became an armed forces recreation camp still in use today. A church building was moved into town for the Methodists. Even after the departure of the military presence in Seward, their effect on the town was long-lasting. Several servicemen stayed, and settled into the community. After the war Seward entered a period of economic downturn, but managed to remain afloat nonetheless.

Induction day in Seward, April 26, 1944, in front of the Seward train depot: Front row, (*left to right*): Gilbert Ollestad, Andrew Peterson, Ralph Neff, Russell Painter. Middle row, (*left to right*): Harry Knutson, Ray Sefrovich, George Hughes, Seward Shea, Seward Prosser. Back row, (*left to right*): John Rose, Hershel Burgin, Wesley Laubsher, Ed Manthey, Cecil Torgramson ("Torgy"), Lloyd Rogers, Ed Estes, Robert Wolfe, Harold Seater. These local servicemen spent the war years working as longshoremen in Seward, Whittier and Dutch Harbor. *Courtesy of Caroline Toloff*

Three members of the 267th Separate Coast Artillery Battalion (Harbor Defense), Battery B, (*left to right*): Walter Lipton, Jack Turnbull and Frank C. Mirabile. The 267th arrived at South Beach (on Caines Head) in December, 1942. Their mission was to reinforce the 250th Coast Artillery (who had arrived in June 1941 to begin construction of the facilities and defenses at South Beach) in order to defend the coast after the Japanese invaded Attu and Kiska. Turnbull, who later became a resident of Seward, worked at the base end station and was a gun pointer on a 155-mm cannon. *Courtesy of Jack Turnbull*

267TH
SEPARATE COAST ARTILLERY BATTALION
(HARBOR DEFENSE)
"Seward's very own Battalion"

The USO building was constructed on Fourth Avenue early in 1942. Servicemen and residents often enjoyed dances and other activities together at the club. *Seward Community Library*

Gordon and Gladys Black, the original owners, in the Dreamland Bowl, 1952. *Courtesy of Kim Kowalski-Rogers*

Photo courtesy of Anchorage Daily News

Kim Kowalski-Rogers, Darrell Rogers, Donna Kowalski, and Marty Kowalski. *Courtesy of Kim Kowalski-Rogers*

The "Dreamland" building was originally erected in 1908 but burned in 1912. The Arctic Brotherhood, a forerunner of the Pioneers of Alaska, rebuilt on the property in 1914. The building was used for numerous businesses over the years including a garage, dance hall, movie theatre during WWII, and finally, for its last 50 years, a bowling alley. The first two lanes of Dreamland Bowl were installed in 1947, with the second pair of lanes going in the following year. Dreamland Bowl was in business from 1948 until it was sold to investors in 1998. Three generations of the Kowalski family owned the business from 1958 until its sale in 1998. The fate of Dreamland Bowl was left up to a fellow who thought he could move the 40' x 100' building and set up business in another spot. The roof was removed, and when the building began its slow trek, it began to fall apart because with the roof absent, the walls were without support. The building did eventually make it to mile 5 of the Seward Highway, where it sat for many years and slowly wasted away to a pile of debris.

Kim Kowalski-Rogers

July 4th in Seward, during World War II.
Seward Community Library

When the local Liberty Theater (owned by Don Carlos Brownell) burned down in February of 1943 the army allowed the townspeople to attend the Dreamland Theater, with the understanding that they had to wait outside whenever Army training films were being screened. This was acceptable to everyone, as the movies were more up-to-date than the Liberty had shown, and only cost ten cents. The new Liberty Theater opened a year later at Third and Adams, its current location (Barry 1995; 162). For the past fifty years the Liberty has been owned and operated by Skip and Marie Fletcher.
Seward Community Library

A raging fire destroyed the east side of Fourth Avenue the night of November 23, 1941. Accidentally started in the Second Chance Barber Shop, the situation worsened as winds fanned the flames. Unwittingly, Army firefighters escalated the fire by trying to dynamite the fire out, which only succeeded in sending burning debris onto neighboring buildings.

Seward Community Library

Ralph Andrews on the steps of his second-hand shop on Fourth Avenue. Andrews, a World War I veteran, began his Army surplus and secondhand business in 1947, starting in a Quonset hut on Fourth Avenue. He continued to expand his operations, and in a few years had the former Alaska House and several warehouses and buildings filled with goods (Barry 1995; 233).

Courtesy of Christina Pichotta

The rebuilt Alaska Shop on Fourth Avenue.
Seward Community Library

H. Everett Hoy, who also went by the moniker "Sourdough Bill," was one of Seward's many eccentric characters. A Navy veteran of World War II, Hoy came to Alaska for a construction job and never left. He chose Seward for his base camp, and was an active member of the American Legion Post #5. In a self-published promotional pamphlet he claims:

"I have prospected, fished, hunted and trapped. I have been butted by mountain goat – pawed by black bear – stomped on by bull moose and bitten by mink. I have done practically everything there is for a man to do in Alaska, for the survival of mind, body and soul. I have danced with the Eskimos and eaten their blubber and rubbed elbos [sic] with the biggest from the Governor to the Secretary of the Interior, from Washington D.C."

Dressing the part, Hoy appeared at various events and conventions as "Sourdough Bill," wearing heavy trousers, parka or plaid shirt, boots and a fur trapper's hat, with a six-shooter at his side. With his long, white beard, Hoy also became a popular Santa Claus around Christmastime (Barry 1995; 267).
Seward Community Library

In preparation for Alaska's admission as the 49th state, the U.S. Congress passed the Alaska Statehood Bill on June 30th, 1958. Seward celebrated the event with a parade, dancing and fireworks (Barry 1995; 231).

Following the bill's passage, a statewide election was held to determine whether Alaska should become a state or remain a territory. The measure passed, and on January 3rd, 1959, President Eisenhower signed the Alaska Statehood Bill.

Impromptu parade on Statehood Day, June 30, 1958.
Courtesy of Chris Warner

Four Cent Fourth of July 1959 Stamp – on this date a 49th star was added to the American flag to represent the new state of Alaska.

1964

The Earthquake

On the evening of Good Friday, March 27, 1964 at 5:36 pm, Seward was rocked by the beginnings of an earthquake which would prove to be the biggest natural disaster the town (and the entire state) had ever experienced. Originating deep under Prince William Sound, multiple shocks registering 8.3 to 8.6 (which have since been upgraded) shook the ground, causing houses to sway and the ground to break into fissures. Down at the waterfront, havoc broke out as the Texaco and Standard Oil storage tanks caught fire, and fully-loaded tanker cars began to explode with a series of terrifying blasts of smoke and flame. Then the seismic waves began. Reaching heights of 30 to 40 feet and spanning the bay, the tsunamis crashed into the shore at speeds of 50 to 60 mph, destroying everything in their path. Train cars and boats were washed away, only to be re-deposited further inland. Railroad tracks were twisted like wire, docks and buildings destroyed, and sections of beachfront land from 50 to

Boat deposited on railroad tracks after the tsunami. *Seward Community Library*

600 feet wide subsided into the bay. All through the night the aftershocks and waves continued. Cars were lined up, packed with people trying to escape the burning town, threading across the narrow lagoon road, only to find the bridge at the Resurrection River unpassable. They turned around, and found refuge at the Bayview school and with the families of Forest Acres subdivision (Barry 1995; 281).

Recovery was a long, slow process, but with the town coming together and aid pouring in from the Red Cross, the U.S. government and individuals all across the globe, order was eventually restored. The Corps of Engineers took over the arduous task of cleaning up the devastation and rebuilding the infrastructure of the town, from sewer and water lines to bridges, roads and docks. Today, forests of "ghost trees" (trees that died as a result of sea water penetrating their roots) can be seen around Resurrection Bay, a grim reminder of the devastating "Good Friday" earthquake.

Oil tanks on the Seward waterfront prior to the 1964 earthquake.
Courtesy of U.S. Army Information Office, Seward Community Library

Smoking remains of Standard Oil tanks after the 1964 earthquake.
Seward Community Library

Bridge and road damage
from the 1964 earthquake.
Seward Community Library

Portion of destroyed
railroad tracks and
dock building after the
earthquake.
Seward Community Library

Sophronia Ballaine Kalin and Florence Ballaine Andrews at the dedication of Ballaine Boulevard during Founders Day Week, 1978. These two daughters of Seward pioneer John Ballaine paid a visit to their hometown during Seward's 75th Anniversary, the Diamond Jubilee. Sophronia Kalin, from Seattle, had last seen Seward in 1914. She majored in physics at college and worked in a radio lab, then as a draftsman. She returned to college, then entered social work. She also authored stories for children's magazines. Her sister, Florence, had left Seward in 1915. She was active in the USO (Barry 1995; 301). In a letter thanking the city for inviting them to the festivities, Sophronia wrote:

"My sister and I never expected to see Alaska again, certainly not under such unusual circumstances. Father would feel highly honored if he could know about it. Seward holds many happy memories for us, such as getting to know the friendly people and meeting interesting visitors from "the outside," gathering columbine and violets on the mountain back of Uncle Frank's house, camping down Resurrection Bay at Porcupine Bay where we feasted on fresh caught salmon, but saw no trace of porcupine, and hiking out to a cabin at Mile Seven for a lunch of brook trout and sourdough pancakes. In many ways this trip will be thrillingly new. Three hours in the air are quite different from six days on the ocean."

Seward Community Library

Aerial photo of Seward, 1965. In the years after the earthquake, Seward went through its ups and downs. The economic base of the town widened, and today counts not only the Alaska Railroad, but several government agencies, a prison, the SeaLife Center, AVTEC (vocational school) and the public school system as providers of stable jobs. Tourism has emerged as a major player as well, helping sustain the town. *Seward Community Library*

TRADITIONS
4th of July

July 4th has a long history of celebration in Seward. In 1903 the pioneers fired off shotguns to celebrate, and a parade has occurred every year since. Contests included pie eating, a greased pole climb, baby contests, the crowning of a Miss Seward and even a beard contest.

Preparing for the annual 4th of July parade.
Seward Community Library

July 4th, circa 1910. Here, the girls of Seward, followed by the Volunteer Fire Department, pass in review before an appreciative crowd. *Seward Community Library*

Seward Community Library

Marching boys in the July 4th parade,
including Howard Romig (*arrow*).
Courtesy of Kerry Romig

Pie eating contest, 1920's.
Seward Community Library

Jr. Women's Club parade float.
Courtesy of Chris Warner

Dodie Fillingim as Lady Liberty and
Bobby Hendricks as Uncle Sam, 1942.
Seward Community Library

Greased pole climb winner.
Courtesy of Seward and Barbara Shea

The centerpiece of Seward's July 4th celebration is the grueling Mt. Marathon Race, which began as a barroom bet in 1915. The original bet claimed no one could climb up to the top of the 3,022 ft. mountain and down again in less than one hour. The winner, James Walters, came close, with a time of 1 hour 2 minutes. By the following year, all three top finishers were able to break the one hour mark. The current record is held by Bill Spencer, who ran a blistering 43:23 in 1981. Today, the race draws hundreds of runners from across the United States (and beyond), and brings thousands of visitors to town.

Six-time race winner Ralph Hatch (*left*) and 1916 winner Alex Bolam, 1964. *Seward Community Library*

Seward's own Ralph Hatch sprinting down Fourth Avenue to win the Mt. Marathon Race in 1947 (clocking in at 58 minutes, 15 seconds). During the late 1940's and early 1950's, Ralph ran the Mt. Marathon race nine times, finishing first six times and second place three times. He is one of an elite few who have won the race multiple times. *Courtesy of Ralph Hatch*

Racers reaching the top.
Seward Community Library

A portion of the
uphill climb on
Mt. Marathon.
Seward Community Library

*Logos courtesy of
Seward Chamber
of Commerce*

SOURCES

Augustine, Lisa (née: Arlene Rheingans). Personal communication, Seward Community Library, August 23, 2002.

Barry, Mary. Seward, Alaska, *A History of the Gateway City.* Volume I, Prehistory to 1914. Anchorage, MJP Barry, 1986.

Barry, Mary. Seward, Alaska, *A History of the Gateway City.* Volume II, 1914-1923 The Railroad Construction Years. Anchorage, MJP Barry, 1993.

Barry, Mary. Seward, Alaska, *A History of the Gateway City.* Volume III, 1924-1993. Growth, Tragedy, Recovery, Adaptation. Anchorage, MJP Barry, 1995.

Bushell, Sharon. "Wilma Lind, Setnets and Chickens," *Anchorage Daily News*, Sunday, April 21, 2002.

Hoy, H. Everett. "Sourdough Bill," Information Unlimited, Seward, Alaska. September 1, 1961, Seward Community Library.

Kalin, Sophronia Ballaine. Personal communication, Seward Community Library, August 6, 1978.

LeVan, Sanna. Personal communication, Seward Community Library.

Mason, Rachel. "Women of Seward – On and Off The Line," Seward History Symposium Proceedings. City of Seward, 2003.

Seward Gateway, October 14, 1911.

PHOTO CREDITS

Alaska State Museum, Juneau, Alaska
Anchorage Daily News
Photos on pages 19, 24, 25, 34, 35, 57, 86, 90 © iStockphoto
Resurrection Bay Historical Society, Seward, Alaska
Seward Chamber of Commerce
Seward Community Library, Seward, Alaska

Margaret Anderson
Lisa Augustine
Doug Capra
Judi Christiansen
Doris P. Fillingim
Karol Gleason
Ralph Hatch
Kim Kowalski-Rogers
Sanna LeVan
Wilma Lind

Vicki Loomis
Christina Pichotta
Kerry Romig
Seward and Barbara Shea
Caroline Toloff
Jack Turnbull
Dorothy Urbach
Chris Warner
Pat Williams